# HOW TO

*Enjoy*

# BEING
# EDITED

*A Practical Guide for*
*Nonfiction Authors*

## HANNAH DE KEIJZER

BELL BUOY PRESS

ISBN (paperback): 979-8-9890079-0-5
ISBN (ebook): 979-8-9890079-1-2

Book design and production by Domini Dragoone
Author photograph by Evan William Smith
Copyedited by Lauren Alexander, proofread by James Gallagher
Cover images: designer's archives; pens © Prapann/AdobeStock

To Dad, for showing me it's possible

to build a life around words

# CONTENTS

INTRODUCTION
**WELCOME, WRITER**............................................... 1

CHAPTER 1
**WHAT EDITORS DO FOR YOUR MANUSCRIPT**........... 9

Coaching..................................................... 10
Revision: Your Own Job....................................... 12
Developmental Editing........................................ 14
Language Editing............................................. 17
Proofreading................................................. 22

CHAPTER 2
**FINDING THE RIGHT EDITOR FOR YOU**.................. 27

Professional Standards....................................... 30
Asking About a Potential Editor's Experience................. 33
Great Fit.................................................... 35

CHAPTER 3
**GETTING THE MOST OUT OF
THE EDITORIAL EXPERIENCE** ............................. 41

Getting the Most Out of a Developmental Edit............... 43
Getting the Most Out of a Language Edit ................... 46

CHAPTER 4

**FEARS AND FAQs**............................................... 51

What will all this cost me? ................................... 51

Are you judging me?.......................................... 53

How do I know when it's time to let go? ...................... 55

How do I know what you've changed in my manuscript?...... 57

Will you rip the heart out of my book?........................ 57


**YOU CAN DO THIS** ............................................ 59


*Resources for a Deeper Dive*


DIVE 1

**SEE FOR YOURSELF: EDITING EXAMPLES**............... 63

Example Developmental Edit ................................. 63

Example Line Edit.......................................... 69

Example Copyedit ........................................ 73

Example Style Sheet ....................................... 75


DIVE 2

**SIX EASY PATHS TO CONNECTION AND SUPPORT**.... 81


DIVE 3

**FOUR REVISION TIPS TO KEEP YOUR READERS
ENTHRALLED—RIGHT TO THE LAST PAGE**.............. 85


DIVE 4

**MORE RESOURCES TO SUPPORT
YOUR BOOK JOURNEY**................................... 91

# WELCOME, WRITER

Writing a book is a labor of effort, creativity, and trust sustained over the long haul. Sneaking words on the page over and over again on your lunch break and after your kids' bedtime. Figuring out what's supposed to happen next as the words coalesce into a manuscript. Wading through a sea of publishing options, choosing one, and following through. Learning how to connect your finished work with the people who will be most excited to read it. So much of this process feels daunting when you're doing it for the first time.

This book exists to take the guesswork out of one essential part of it, the part that helps get you from idea to draft to publishable text: having your book edited.

> Editing is about working with professionals to nourish your manuscript and shepherd it to its very best form—while at the same time reenergizing you, the writer, with fresh curiosity and excitement for your book.

If the idea of being edited makes you hot-potato slide your manuscript in a drawer and drop into a defensive crouch, or conjures images of nasty comments scribbled in the margins of your hard work, consider this your formal invitation into a different vision. Here, your editors are partners by your side.

Before the COVID-19 pandemic, my husband and I loved to host. He's an academic; most of our friends at the time were, too. Every semester I'd watch their gripe-o-meters and stress-o-meters nudge higher and higher until, by grading time, my friends were little more than exhausted, groaning husks of themselves. So we applied our love of hosting to our community's shared need for both emotional support and practical accomplishment: we opened our home for grading nights at the end of each semester.

The invite was simple. Our door would be open between 5:00 and 11:00 p.m. on Tuesday. Come whenever, leave whenever. We put snacks out or everyone went in on a food order or folks brought nibbles and beer. Friends plopped themselves down around the table or on the couch or by the fire. We talked and laughed a bit, but were usually good about leaving each other alone. So much was accomplished in one night. And it felt so good.

That's the feeling I want for you as you write. That feeling of being held up and given energy by friends. Of being cozy by a fire. Of being delighted by how much you can accomplish with company. This book is an offering to that end.

Working with editors isn't automatically that, of course (and unfortunately). But it can be—and I'll walk you through exactly how to make it possible. If you're a new or new-ish author, this book will help you understand what editors really do. You'll be able to choose editors who will do right by you and your manuscript and to feel confident and capable as you work together. If you've published before, this book will guide you toward an even more useful and fulfilling editorial experience. No matter where you are in your career as a writer, let the information here help you publish books you're thrilled to see your name on—with less heartache along the way.

**Chapter 1** describes the different types of editing and discusses when in your manuscript's life each is most useful. Use the handy-dandy flowchart on the following page as a map. It gives you a preview of how a manuscript moves through the editorial process over time and lets you identify which sections of the book might be most relevant to you right now.

**Chapter 2** is a guide to finding professional editors and figuring out who will be a terrific match for you and your particular book.

Once you've found them, use the tips and prompts in **Chapter 3** to get the most out of working together.

**Chapter 4** covers common questions and fears about the editorial process, like how much it costs and whether or not your editor is judging you. (Spoiler alert: we're not.)

At the end of the book you'll find **Resources** to help you dive deeper, including examples of the different types of editing in action.

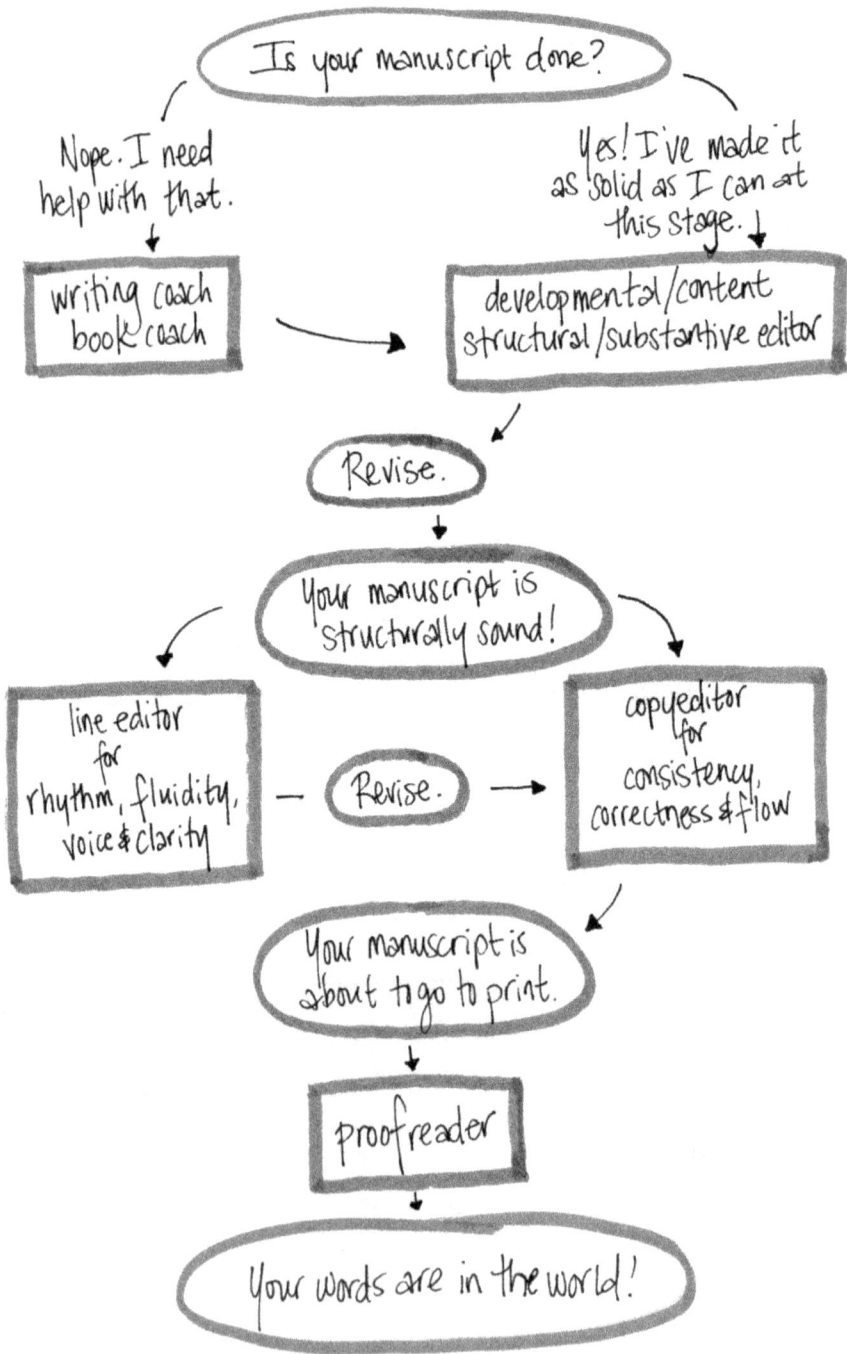

Is your manuscript done?

Nope. I need help with that.

Yes! I've made it as solid as I can at this stage.

writing coach
book coach

developmental/content
structural/substantive editor

Revise.

Your manuscript is structurally sound!

line editor for rhythm, fluidity, voice & clarity

Revise.

copyeditor for consistency, correctness & flow

Your manuscript is about to go to print.

proofreader

Your words are in the world!

Because in-house editors at publishing companies are almost never available to edit other books, I focus on the independent professionals you can hire directly. That makes this guide especially useful for those of you who are self-publishing—aka independently publishing. But it's relevant for traditionally published authors, too.

If you're aiming for traditional publishing, your publisher *should* provide editing—ideally all along the way but at least a round of copyediting and a round of proofreading. It's your responsibility as the author to make sure these are in your contract and to find independent professionals to do those jobs if your publisher does not. For example, authors have called on me to do early edits on scholarly manuscripts under contract with an academic press so they could submit as sound a text as possible. Others have tapped me to proofread a manuscript right before it went to print because they wanted that essential last outside eye to catch lingering errors.

This book will be your companion as you fill in the gaps of your publisher's support. It'll also help you know what questions to ask to get the most out of all your editorial partnerships, whether in-house or independent.


## BUT DO YOU REALLY NEED AN EDITOR?

Short answer: yes. Even if you're not yet ready to believe in the possibility of editor as ally, here are some practical reasons why it's worth working with one.

### Your audience has expectations.

Frankly, readers are used to certain standards of readability and correctness, and often like to be vocal in online reviews about any deviation from those standards. A book that reads well is much more likely to be recommended to friends and colleagues. The bar is high. An editor helps you leap right over it.

### Your reputation is on the line.

As a nonfiction writer, you might be writing to solidify your reputation in your field or to directly advance your career. Hello speaking gigs, hello media coverage, hello tenure file. The book shouldering this burden should be published at its very best, and an editor—along with your diligent, curious revising—can get it there.

### Your reader deserves an early advocate.

You're an expert in your own story, ideas, research, or business. Your readers cannot know everything you know, but it's hard to put yourself in their shoes when you're writing. Editors help you make sure readers will stay engaged start to finish by flagging where you're making too many assumptions or leaving out crucial information that readers actually need.

### You want to be proud of your book.

You want your book to reflect you in all the most flattering ways. (If that weren't true, I don't think you'd be bothering to read this one.) Your editors want that, too, and have the professional training, expertise, and experience to help make it happen. Your book will be better written and more compelling after working with a good editor.

### You'll become a better writer.

A good editor celebrates your delicious sentences and your beautiful arguments. They remind you of the current strengths of your writing and your manuscript. They also show you where your book can be improved—and how to do it. That means each edit is an opportunity to build your writing skill, if you want it to be.

**You deserve a break.**

Handing the manuscript off to your editor gives you a well-earned break, permission not to think about your work for a while. When they return it to you, you can review, incorporate, and revise in response to the edits on your own time. Their ideas, combined with the fresh perspective and renewed energy you get from time away from the work, can develop your manuscript in a tremendously exciting way.

· · ·

I've been editing nonfiction for over fifteen years—everything from leadership guides to law texts, artist statements to memoir—for independent authors and business owners, arts organizations, a skincare company, a nonprofit, a government initiative.

> Witnessing the boost of energy and ideas when writers receive their freshly edited manuscripts just doesn't get old. I've seen over and over again how much it fuels writers—and you need lots of fuel to get all the way from having an idea to publishing a book!

Ready to get some of that fuel yourself, and find out everything editing can do for you? Read on.

# CHAPTER 1

# WHAT EDITORS DO FOR YOUR MANUSCRIPT

You know you want to write a book, but you have absolutely no idea how to wrangle the explosion of thoughts in your head into something coherent. Or you started writing, but now you've stalled out and the words are...elusive. Or the word count keeps ticking up but you're desperately wishing for an easier or less lonely way to get this book done.

First: there is no shame in this. You're not the only one. Many people struggle to finish their drafts, whether it's due to mindset, current skill, not knowing what to tackle next, lack of time, dwindling interest, or the simple fact that writing is often hard and writing a whole book is even harder. But I'm cheering for you to finish that draft, get all the way through the publishing process, and see your book in a happy reader's hands.

So here's the good news: you don't have to do it alone, and thinking you do could be what's keeping you stuck.

Pardon me while I climb onto my soapbox for a moment to say that there's an extra cost to struggling by ourselves because we think we "should" be able to do it alone. Alongside our difficulty with the project itself, we often accumulate a load of guilt and shame that only digs us deeper into the hole. Thinking openly and creatively about what kind of help we need, and screwing up the courage to ask for that help, is freeing. The brain space! The sudden energy for the actual work we want to do!

The first, easiest way out of the hole is looking for support inside your community or widening your community to include more fellow writers who are committed to finishing their own work. Free options to help you bring your manuscript to life include writing groups, critique partners, coworking sessions with friends, and accountability buddies. See Dive 2 at the back of this book for a list of easy ideas to build the connection and support that nourish you and your writing for the long haul. Now, off the soapbox and back to the regularly scheduled programming of publishing professionals.

## COACHING

Who can help you get from idea to finished draft? A ghostwriter will assemble the words for you. But if you want to be the full author of your own book, turn to writing coaches and book coaches. The job of a coach is to question, jiggle, explore, celebrate, bring forth, and crack open in service of you getting clear on your ideas and creating really good bones for your book. They will ask so many questions. They'll poke holes. They should explicitly appreciate what's already working and what's unique about you and your project. They may send you back to the beginning. And

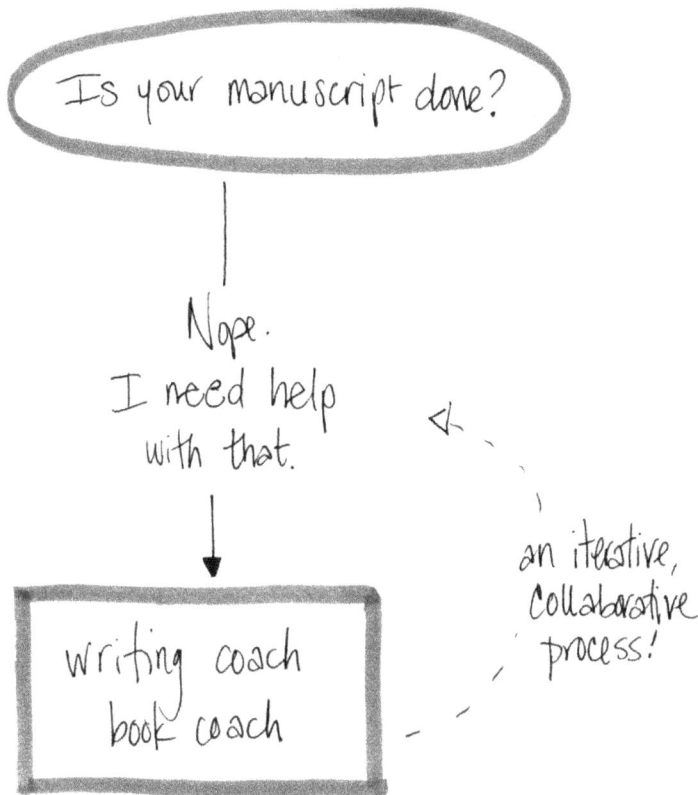

Is your manuscript done?

Nope.
I need help
with that.

writing coach
book coach

an iterative,
collaborative
process!

they'll get you to the end by helping you develop a concrete plan and keeping you accountable to it.

Lots of people call themselves coaches. Before beginning work with someone, consider what you need help with and why. Think about how you usually learn best and what circumstances and relationships let you do your best work. As you approach possible coaches, make sure you're clear on what services they offer and how that aligns with what you need. Though if you don't *know* why you're stuck or what will help you, that's OK, too—the coach is there to guide you in figuring it out!

Some writing coaches focus on process and mindset, while others give feedback on or even edit your actual writing. Some, like me, do both. Some book coaches concern themselves primarily with structure and main ideas, while others offer more micro-level guidance. Some offer one-off services or hourly coaching, while others do only durational programs or packages. Some ease your way from concept to outline, some help you get unstuck in the middle of the process, and others help you research the market or draw up a list of potential publishers. What will work best for you?

Your needs may change over time. Find a coach with the skill range to shift with you, or thank one coach for their help and find someone else for your next phase. A good coach or editor will always be responsive and invested in giving you what you need to succeed. They should release you without pressure if their expertise and your work are no longer a good fit. Just make sure you've paid them before you go.

Who you choose to work with should be a matter of their experience, expertise, and credibility, as well as the fit between you, your field or genre, your process, and what they're offering. Chapter 2 is full of advice on how to find a great match.

## REVISION: YOUR OWN JOB

When your first draft is done, celebrate! You conquered the blank page, probably pushed past a lot of anxiety and self-doubt, and managed to get your ideas down on paper. This is an accomplishment in and of itself.

After you take the time to appreciate how amazing it is that you just drafted a book, put the manuscript away and don't look at it for a little while. I like a month or so apart, so I can come back with fresh eyes. If a week is all you can spare, take a week. I've heard some writers say they put it away for six months or even a year (though I'd worry about this sapping momentum in a nonfiction process). We've all heard the stories of manuscripts long buried in desk drawers pulled out years later and turned into masterpieces. You'll figure out the rhythms that work for you. Whatever amount of time you take, your writing will benefit from a short hiatus and the perspective it gives you.

Come back to your manuscript ready to dig in deeply. It's time for revision! Clarify your arguments and draw out your voice. Make sure you're clear on who you're writing for—perhaps enlist beta readers at this stage to get a reader's perspective on what you might be missing. Add the critical research you forgot the first time. Cut what doesn't support your real point (see Dive 3 in the back of the book for more on this and other revision tips).

Wait—isn't this what an editor does? Yes, it can be. But there's no getting off the hook here.

> An editor's work is not a substitute for your own deep engagement with and careful revision of your manuscript. It's a support.

So revise your own first draft, and revise again. When you start to feel you've hit a wall, worry you're pushing your book in the wrong direction, or are just ready for an outside perspective, you'll know it's time to hire an editor to work with the complete draft from the big-picture perspective.

## DEVELOPMENTAL EDITING

Who do you turn to for these first edits on a revised draft? Developmental/structural/substantive/content editors. Editors might label themselves and their services with any of these terms—I know, I know—but these labels all refer to editing at the macro, structural level. I'll use "developmental editing" going forward because that's what I call my own work in this category. Developmental editors make suggestions inside the context of the whole manuscript, knowing how each part works, or could work, together.

> We're making the foundation and structural supports solid so you can build a house of clear, compelling writing on top of them.

You can also think of your developmental editor as a master trail designer. You call them in to help set a clear, well-signed, continuous path for your reader, sited comfortably in the terrain and fully filled so no major holes remain. Why bother? If the manuscript's path is a series of disconnected patches, your reader might get lost or decide it's not worth the effort to bushwhack from one to the next. Bushwhacking is tiring, after all! Or if the path is full of holes—places the reader is asking questions that don't get answered—they might get confused, bored, or frustrated. Lost, confused, or frustrated readers are much more likely to give up and put your book down before they reach the end.

Is your manuscript done?

|

Yes! I've made it
as solid as I can at this
stage.

↓

Celebrate!
Put it away for a
little while.

↓

Revise.    ▷ beta readers
possible here

↓

developmental/content/
structural/substantive
editor

sometimes an
iterative
process ↗

↓

Revise.

↖ sensing a theme?

Though the turnaround time for a developmental edit varies, a month is about average. The developmental edit comes back to you in the form of an *editorial memo*, also known as a *revision letter*. This hearty document—often ten to twenty pages—contextualizes and explains in detail any edits in the manuscript. It discusses overall themes, broad concerns, and celebration-worthy aspects of your work. It also offers concrete suggestions for how to move the manuscript forward.

Developmental editors usually provide only minimal work inside the manuscript; that work skews more toward comments highlighting ideas from the revision letter than toward careful word edits in the text itself. After all, if you're going to do a major overhaul of the structure, your writing will likely change alongside it. It doesn't make sense to spend time massaging the perfect sentence if that sentence isn't going to be in the manuscript next month. Always ask your own editor what you can expect from their particular method.

Working with a developmental editor is especially powerful as an iterative process, with the editing and revising focusing on increasingly detailed aspects of the work each time. If you and your editor want it to be, the process can be a sustained collaboration that's more like coaching and idea development. In fact, independent editors who do developmental work in this way often call that work coaching. (This is what many folks picture when they think of ye olde white male editors at big publishing houses nurturing now-famous texts from draft to book. Many editors at publishing houses still work this way.)

> No matter what, though, a heads-up: incorporating editorial feedback at this level will entail major revisions. And your book will be stronger for it!

If this service is more than you or your budget can take on right now, consider a *manuscript critique* (aka *manuscript assessment* or *manuscript evaluation*), which is a one-pass commentary on your book. Assessments like this are much more common for fiction than nonfiction, but some nonfiction editors do offer them. You'll likely get back a much shorter editorial memo responding to the book as a whole but no editorial work in the manuscript itself. This service usually costs significantly less than a full developmental edit. (See Chapter 4 for more on cost.)

## LANGUAGE EDITING

So now you've written your book, revised it, received big-picture support from a developmental editor, and revised it again in response. Your arguments are solid. The main components of your text are in a logical order. Maybe you've sent it to some beta readers who exemplify your ideal audience and have incorporated the feedback that showed up consistently in their responses. What comes next?

## Line Editing

Does this book sound like *you*? Does each sentence and paragraph flow well into the next, linking your ideas clearly? Does it march, pop off the page, shine or shimmer, glide or flow in the way you want? Are the tone and quality of writing consistent, with enough rhythmic variation to keep your reader awake and attentive? Are you choosing words that your intended reader will absorb without feeling either patronized or overwhelmed?

To make sure, call a line editor, sometimes called a stylistic editor—friend of fluidity, rhythm, and readability. They will go line by line, word by word, helping you make your ideas and your particular voice shine. Many people skip this level of editing because they're confident in their own voice and writing skills or because of time or budgetary constraints. If that's you, fair enough. I'm a line editor, so I'm obviously biased, but I think this is the stage of editing that most helps your writing be both inviting and memorable.

Line editing is the process of cleaning the last branches from your book's path so nobody will trip and picking just the right beautiful stones for borders and bridges. We're setting comfortable benches along the way so folks who get tired have a place to rest without leaving the path. We're planting wildflowers and clearing moments for a remarkable vista. Everything that will make readers want to keep walking—and recommend this walk to friends.

After working with a line editor, you'll revise, revise, revise. Are you sensing a theme? Then...

Your manuscript is structurally sound!

line editor for rhythm, fluidity, voice & clarity

Revise.

copy editor for consistency, correctness & flow

Surprise! You check, but don't really revise.

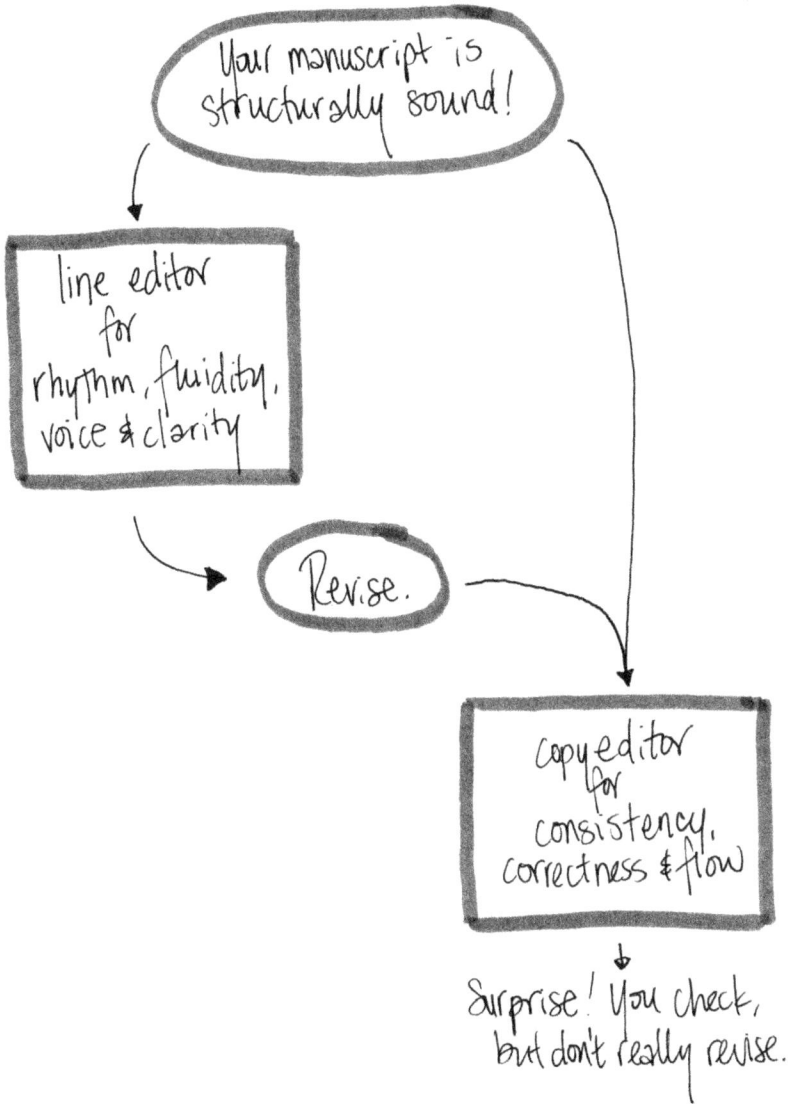

If needed, see also: fact-checker, sensitivity reader, and/or technical editor.

## Copyediting

Are all your details accurate and consistent? Like, really, *all* your details? Are your grammar and punctuation in order? Even if you're choosing to bend convention, someone else has to make sure you've done so consistently. I guarantee you're too close to the manuscript to see it yourself.

To make sure, call a copyeditor—friend of cleanliness, correctness, and concision.

> May we all bow down to the good copyeditors of the world, thoughtful and knowledgeable folks who guide your manuscript into shape on usage, internal consistency of facts and details, grammar, and spelling.

Copyeditors are the ones who catch when you've mismatched a date and day of the week, even though you've checked three times. Or notice that you describe someone driving south along an avenue in New York that's really a one way in the opposite direction. Copyediting is essential cleanup.

Some line editors (like me) include elements of copyediting in their service. Some copyeditors include attention to flow and voice in their copyedit (like Lauren, my editor for this book)—then usually called a *heavy* copyedit. As always, talk to your own potential editor to find out what depth of edit they can offer. If you're not sure exactly what level of language editing will most benefit your manuscript, trust an editor to guide you.

Note that excellent copyeditors are experts in the conventional style guides—for books it's often *The Chicago Manual of Style*—and know exactly where to look up their questions. But they're also flexible enough to chuck those rules out the window when they don't serve your manuscript. This tricky blend of expertise and flexibility is part of why copyediting is a job for professionals. An experienced copyeditor—and proofreader, for that matter—will strengthen your manuscript for marketplace viability in a way that you or your friendly former English teacher just can't.

*Style guides*, mentioned above, are essentially the rule books. *Style sheets*, on the other hand, are simple repository documents for your book's particular details and idiosyncrasies. The style sheet for this book includes that I prefer "OK" to "okay," for example. Your copyeditor will create a style sheet to record your preferences and their editorial decisions. This helps them stay consistent and shows the proofreader and designers what the publishing team has already agreed on. If you're publishing independently, the style sheet buck stops at you and your copyeditor. If you're publishing with a traditional or hybrid press, your publisher will have a *house style* to which your copyeditor must align your manuscript; you may or may not be able to negotiate with the publisher on some choices.

All language edits come back to you by way of detailed changes and notes in the manuscript itself. Most editors use the Track Changes feature in Microsoft Word to show you what they've done and to leave questions, comments, and explanations in the margins. It's then up to you to accept or reject the editor's changes.

> After line editing, there's still plenty of room for revision, but copyediting is usually a final touch-up.

If you revise after a copyedit, you may be undoing your editor's very hard work, introducing new errors, and driving everyone wild. Please don't do that to yourself or your publishing team! If you really, truly, absolutely need to make a change after the copyedit, consider doing so with Track Changes turned on and reaching out to your copyeditor to ask for a review of the changed material.

Other important kinds of editing usually used around the time of this language-focused work include:

- Sensitivity editing for bias, inclusivity, and accuracy to the lived experience of a group to which you may not belong.

- Technical editing for technical correctness of instruction manuals and the like.

- Fact-checking, which is often lumped in with copyediting but is actually a separate, critical task for some books.

Editors may combine these types of editing with a copyediting service; ask yours about it.

## PROOFREADING

This section could just as easily be called "What You Don't Know Is Wrong Until It's Too Late." I write an email newsletter about writing, revision, editing, and shaping a sustainable writing practice. One issue arrived in inboxes with a word missing from line two. I accidentally sent another with a whole section appearing twice. We're all too close to our own work to catch the mistakes *every* time, even the professionals.

Your book is done —
and awesome!
It's about to go to print.

↓

proofreader

↓

Your words are in the
world in their best possible
form!

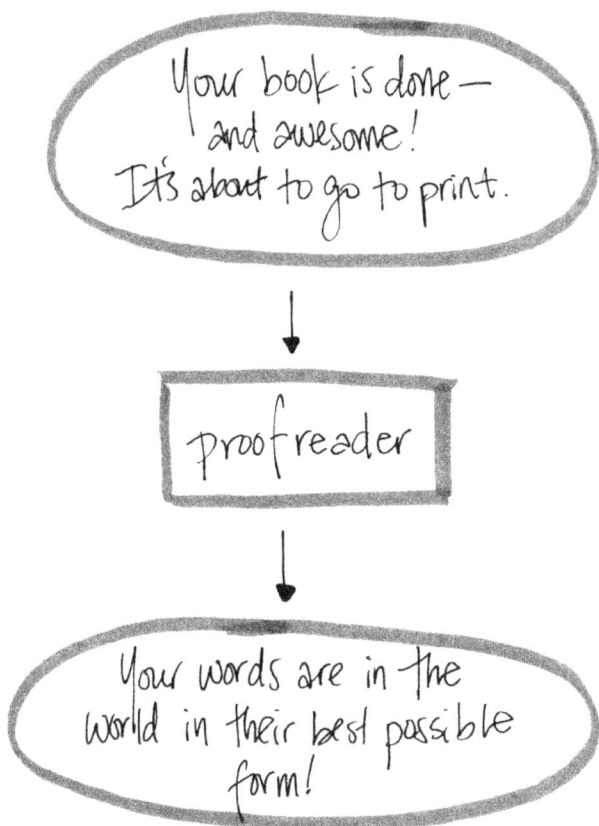

If needed, see also: indexer.

When you already have a good relationship with your audience, it's easier to let go of moments like my missing-word goof. But what about when this is your first—or only—chance to impress a reader? What if you're trying to avoid the online reviews where people dock stars for too many typos? What if you believe, as I do, that to give your work its best chance in the world, the presentation has to live up to the prose?

> Hire a proofreader. Their job is to scrub your book squeaky clean so you look maximally professional and the reader's attention stays on your ideas, not your slipups.

The proofreader is the last person standing between your audience and that sentence that says "can" where it should say "can't" or "starts" where it should say "stars." They catch where you cited legal rule 112(b) when you meant 112(6)—still my proudest proofreading moment. The proofreader's fresh eyes on your work at the last stage not only help you avoid typos that distract or hamper your reader, but also help you catch potentially embarrassing or disqualifying errors. Proofreader Matthew Webster-Moore shares this story:

> I proofread reports for lawyers dealing with medical negligence cases. The medical experts who write these reports rely on their own knowledge and on specific clinical guidelines when supporting their evidence for any "breaches of duty" by the hospital or care home in question. Whatever guidelines are used in their report must be in place at the time of the incident, otherwise that evidence could be discounted in court. Not long ago one of the experts used a guideline that was published a month after the incident. When I flagged that, they had to revise their report but were very grateful the evidence wouldn't be automatically dismissed!

The traditional use of the term proofreading refers to the process of ensuring all the copyedits were successfully transferred to the final layouts of your book. More commonly these days, proofreaders do a *cold read* on final page proofs to minimize the chances of any stray errors making it into your book. This includes spotting formatting mistakes, like headers appearing on the last line of a page or an image being misaligned; checking image and figure captions; and confirming the chapter titles and page numbers in the table of contents match what's actually in the book. Yes, errors in those details may have snuck past everyone else or gone wrong at the last minute.

In developmental and line editing, I'm listening deeply, reading closely, and imagining in your voice and vision. But when I'm proofreading, I cut myself off from you and your words. Through most of the process, I'm not even reading for understanding. Instead I'm breaking down words, reading syllable by syllable out loud, looking at the shapes of lines on the page, and calling on my style guide knowledge to check punctuation and citations. The exception comes when I think I've found a mistake; I zoom out and really read the sentence or paragraph to double-check the intended meaning. If your reader has to keep double-checking, you're in trouble.

If your book needs an index, you'll probably also be hiring an indexer at this very last stage of the process, as their work requires final page numbers. Don't wait until the last minute to approach either proofreaders or indexers, though. You need at least a few weeks' heads-up to send out feelers, receive quotes, and be penciled in on their calendar.

· · ·

One final note on cleaning up the text: you're a smart and capable human, but you're also very familiar with your work. You've been staring at this book, draft after draft, for months or years. And it's this very familiarity that disqualifies you from being your own proofreader—or copyeditor, frankly. Corinne Jorgenson, a cognitive scientist and teacher of cognitive psychology at the University of Cincinnati, explains it this way:

> Writing is an incredibly complex mental and physical process. Fortunately, we're rarely aware of the many steps our brain takes to turn a thought into an email, a paragraph, a book. It just kind of happens, as if by magic.
>
> That magic is called a mental map. We use mental maps all the time to generalize complex tasks—when we write emails, as we shower, even while we drive to work. And when you reread your writing, your attention is divided between your mental map of the work and the actual words on the screen. Your brain knows what it meant to say, and this powerful mental model often wins the competition for your attention. That's why it's so hard to see errors on the screen or page.

So if you want your book to be as clean as it can possibly be, hand it over to a professional for that final check.

# CHAPTER 2

# FINDING THE RIGHT EDITOR FOR YOU

N ow that you're familiar with the different levels of editing and when you might use them, how do you go about finding the right editor(s) for you? There are two main components to this. You need someone who can deliver edits to professional standards, of course, on time and within your budget. But fundamentally you also want someone who will do right by you and your work. Someone who will empower you and give you confidence in your manuscript as it develops.

> That's the key to you enjoying the editorial process, and it's a matter of process and feelings fit as much as one of professional skill.

We'll tackle both components here.

After you've read this book, done your searches, and made a list of promising potential editors, select two or three especially appealing candidates and send them an email. Book a free connection or discovery call, if they offer that option. Having a written and verbal conversation is the best way to get a sense of what it's like to actually work with them.

Most editors will want to see your full manuscript before agreeing to work with you (coaches don't need this, of course). It's not because we're out to steal your ideas. It's not a judgment process, either. Seeing the manuscript is the only way we get an honest sense of how your whole text reads. (Because if you're only sending a single chapter, it's probably the most polished one, right?) It lets us provide an accurate service fee. And, since most language editors provide a sample edit on a few thousand words, sharing your manuscript now can give you a valuable chance to see the editor at work. Do you like how they express their suggestions? Do they seem to match your voice well? If you hate all your editor's suggestions in the sample, you'll probably hate all their suggestions in the full edit, too—so look elsewhere.

Some editors do the sample edit for free. Some charge a small fee that, if you decide to work with them, is folded into the final service fee. Even if you end up working with someone else, though, a paid sample edit isn't money wasted. It gives you a piece of professionally generated material to learn from and helps you refine your own taste around what kind of editorial feedback is most useful. Note: it's basically impossible to do a sample for a developmental edit because of the nature of the work, so you'll want to rely on testimonials and ask lots of questions—see Chapter 3 for help.

Seeing your manuscript up front is also a fit check on the editor's end. If you think your manuscript just needs a proofread but the editor sees that the sentences are still choppy or the argument is hard to follow, they're going to recommend backing up a step or two. An ethical editor uses this moment to check whether your manuscript is right for them in other ways, too. Maybe it deals with a subject too personal or emotionally fraught for the editor to handle objectively. I haven't always been in a place to take on cancer memoirs, for example. Maybe they don't have the skills needed to move your book forward. If it's not a good fit for them, they should speak up about it. Some editors might even recommend a colleague who could be a better match.

Be sure to approach your potential editors well in advance if at all possible—at least a couple of weeks for proofreading and up to several months for developmental and language editing. Many editors schedule projects in advance, and while you may get lucky and your favorite editor could happen to have a gap in their schedule exactly when you contact them, do you want to risk that?

I know it can feel scary to open your manuscript to an editor before you feel it's ready, but editors won't think less of you. Indeed, they'll appreciate your respect for their schedule. And having an editorial agreement booked on a certain date can be a wonderful motivator for getting the writing done and letting the darn thing go!

If timing can't be helped and you're looking for a quick turnaround, most editors rightly charge a rush fee. Quality should take precedence over speed whenever possible. Good editing takes time. And keep in mind that different types of editing take longer than others—for example, developmental edits take longer than proofreads—so plan accordingly.

## PROFESSIONAL STANDARDS

To find someone who can work to professional standards, which should include getting work in on time, turn first to professional associations for editors. Much of an editor's training happens through these organizations. Members are also usually more active in the field. They're more likely to be up on current trends in usage, edit with conscious style in mind, and have a network of colleagues they can turn to for advice. These are all signs of a professional editor who cares about the quality of their work, and yours. I'm a member of both the Editorial Freelancers Association and ACES: The Society for Editing, and am constantly grateful for the continuing education and community they provide.

When you get to an organization's member database, search for the level of editing you need and the genre of your material, or just browse to explore who's out there. This list of databases focuses on countries whose primary language is English, but excellent editors abound globally. Unless your book has specific bilingual needs, I usually recommend finding an editor who is a native speaker of the language you'll be publishing in—if you're writing primarily for the Australian market, for example, try to find an Australian editor who will fully understand that country's usage nuances. That said, many editors edit in more than one language or can proofread in both British English and American English, for example; if they're the right person for you based on other rubrics of fit detailed later in this section, go for it.

## Professional Organizations with
## Searchable Membership Databases

The links to these organizations' membership databases are accessible via Dive 4 at the back of the book.

ACES: The Society for Editing (United States)

Club Ed (primarily United States)

Editorial Freelancers Association (United States)

Editors of Color (United States)

American Society for Indexing (United States)

Association of Canadian Publishers (Canada)

Editors Canada (Canada)

The Institute of Professional Editors (Australia and New Zealand)

Association of Freelance Editors, Proofreaders & Indexers of Ireland (Ireland)

Chartered Institute of Editing and Proofreading (United Kingdom)

You can also track editors down by checking the acknowledgment sections of books you admire in your genre. Google any editors mentioned by name to discover if they work for the publisher or are freelance and therefore may be available to edit your book, too. Ask fellow writers and colleagues for recommendations. If the editor they endorse doesn't do the kind of work your manuscript needs right now, you can always save the contact information for a later phase of your book or for a future one.

You can also follow the online platforms of writers, editors, writing organizations, and publishing professionals. Pay attention to public conversations and reviews around books in your genre. You'll either directly find editors whose ideas and process you respect, or learn of editors through those other professionals. You'll certainly pick up on additional ways of thinking about writing craft, revision, and editing, as well as on the kinds of questions that will help you get the most out of your edits. (For more on maximizing your experience of working with an editor, see Chapter 3.)

## Professional Credentials for Coaches

Note that there aren't professional organizations for writing coaches and book coaches in the same way there are for editors. Though coaching courses and a couple of reputable coaching certification programs do exist, like the Author Accelerator program, much of a book coach's training is informal or experiential. This doesn't mean they can't be powerfully effective, but don't be shy about reading testimonials and asking careful questions so you know what kind of support and experience you're getting into.

## Freelance Marketplaces

What about freelance service marketplaces? Many reputable editors do hang out a virtual shingle on Reedsy. Upwork and Fiverr are possible options if you're on a budget and want to find a newer editor looking for experience who may charge less. Depending on where in the world you live, these sites may be the primary available means of finding and hiring freelance editors. But these sites are also full of people who charge you money only to under-deliver or harm your work. Please, please approach these sites with extreme caution.

> Don't lunge at the cheapest quote. Check credentials carefully, ask for a sample edit and testimonials, speak with references if you can, inspect the published versions of the work in their portfolio to see if you think it's well written and edited…

…and follow all the other guidance in this chapter.

## ASKING ABOUT A POTENTIAL EDITOR'S EXPERIENCE

Here are some questions you can ask potential editors to get a sense of their experience level and whether you think they'll deliver edits that will improve your book.

### What kind(s) of editing do you offer, or specialize in?

As you now know, editors may label their work differently, but the basic levels of editing are the same. They should be able to talk to you about what level their work falls into and discuss what they pay attention to within that category. An editor thinking about overall structure, order of ideas, and whether you've included the right information for your intended audience, for example, is working as a substantive or developmental editor, not a copyeditor. Note: many editors edit at more than one level—just not at the same time.

**What's your training?**

**Have you worked on books like mine before?**

**What kind of work do you love editing?**

Many paths can bring someone to being a good editor, all marked by a commitment to studying the craft and nuances of editing itself. Maybe the editor worked in the publishing industry for a while and has gone freelance. Maybe they just worked their way into it over time, accumulating training, experience, and expertise as they went. Both are legit. It's a good sign if the editor is a member of a professional editing organization and continues to take courses, as discussed above. A serious editor is always learning more about their craft.

If an editor has already worked on thirty published books in your category, you can be confident you're getting someone who knows what they're doing. (Whether they're the right editor *for you* is a separate question, addressed in the next section.) If an editor is new to the field but has undergone substantive training, it's worth giving them a chance by seeing a sample edit. Your budget may thank you for it, as editors rightly increase their prices as they gain experience and years in business.

There's no reason to immediately rule someone out if they're not a specialist in your genre or field. If your intended readers are less experienced than you, an editor who is not an expert in your field can be a perfect liaison between you and your readers. Since an editor is also a reader advocate, it can be useful to have a competent nonspecialist editor highlighting the areas of your manuscript where lay readers will stumble. Just make sure the editor can talk convincingly about how their experience will translate effectively to working with your book.

**You probably *should* rule someone out if you notice any of these red flags:** "Reading a lot" isn't enough to make someone a good editor. Loving books isn't enough. An English degree alone isn't enough, and many excellent editors don't have one, myself included. Being interested in editing isn't enough. Being told by their friends, colleagues, or local volunteer organization that they have an eye for detail and would make a good editor isn't enough. Having written a book themselves isn't enough. If these are the only credentials they can offer, please don't hire one of these folks to help you. They may be well intentioned, or they may not be; either way, you won't be getting the best edit for your money, nor the best possible final book.

### Do you have testimonials or references?

Editors usually have testimonials on their website or will provide them upon request. They might also be willing to connect you to past clients directly so you can hear more about the client experience. The language in testimonials also gives you clues into an editor's process and what working with that person *feels* like—both important parts of finding the right editor for you. Let's get into that now.

## GREAT FIT

You stand a much better chance of enjoying the editing process if you're guided through it by someone you genuinely click with. You deserve to work with an editor who is clear and communicative about their process, and whose process fits *your* brain and preferred ways of working. Open communication is especially helpful when you're working with an editor for the very first time and want to know what to expect as you go along.

Here are some specific aspects of fit to keep in mind or to ask your potential editor about during introductory conversations. Use them as an alignment check on both practicalities and vibe.

## Do our logistical needs align?

There are lots of details to agree to in the beginning, and the ease with which you two do so is a good indicator of what your working relationship will be like throughout. You also need to be willing and able to do what the editor asks for in getting set up. Do they require a signed service agreement or contract, which is always a good idea for big jobs and new relationships, or is an email agreement enough? Do you reserve their time with only a signed service agreement, with a deposit payment, or with full payment up front? What format do they want the manuscript in, and how will they return the edits to you? Are there any editorial or payment milestones you should know about? And what will be delivered at the end? How will you both know the editor's work is complete? For example, some language editors include with their standard service a cleanup round of editing; they do an initial edit, you revise, and then they do a final check and polish. Some editors may be willing to add this onto their service for an additional fee, even if it's not standard. Some may not.

Aligning expectations about all these logistics up front keeps the working relationship smooth and mutually supportive. It also helps you stay relaxed throughout the editing process.

## Do our communication needs and styles align?

First things first: Do you two like communicating by the same means? If you hate appearing on camera, avoid the coach who only works via Zoom. If you prefer to receive questions via text because your inbox is so full it makes you panic, your editor needs to know that up front.

Copyeditor Lori Paximadis tells potential clients her own needs right from the start: "I get that there are people out there who love to chat and hash things out on the phone, but it's really uncomfortable and awkward and draining and time consuming for me. If an author needs to have phone conversations, I'm simply not the right editor for them and they are not the right client for me, full stop. That doesn't make either of us bad at what we do; we're just not the right fit."

Communication fit isn't just about whether you like chatting over email or phone. What expectations do you have of each other through the process? If you want project updates as they work, are they willing to provide some? Do you want your editor to email you every time a question about the work arises, or just send one or two compiled lists? Are you looking for a collaborative, back-and-forth conversation with your editor, or would you rather hear nothing until you're sent a polished manuscript with minimal questions and notes in the margins? Do you prefer direct suggestions about what you need to cut or change, or would you like everything phrased as a suggestion or invitation? Do you want the chance to talk through the changes with the editor directly after they're done? If this is your first time working with an editor, you may not know the answers to these questions yet. That's fine! Use conversations with potential editors to begin to find out.

## Do we want the same thing from the relationship and from this edit?

If you're looking for an editor to help you develop your craft, you may want someone who will suggest changes but leave them for you to execute so you're building your chops. You may want as many explanations as possible so you understand why the editor makes the changes and suggestions they do. On the other hand, if you're ready to get this book over with, you might want to be told exactly what to do to "fix" the manuscript. Or you may just want the text cleaned up so it's ready to go with as little future engagement from you as possible. What feels most appealing to you at this stage? Remember you'll have a break from the manuscript while it's with your editor, so don't let being sick of the text right now completely dictate your choices. Talk through your preferences with your editor and find out if what you want is a match with what they can provide.

## Does this person feel like someone you can enjoy working with, and whom you can trust to do well by you and your work?

It's OK—great, even—to keep looking until you find an editor who fits you. You want someone you enjoy interacting with. Someone who listens carefully to you and your goals for the book and is committed to making your writing shine in its uniqueness.

Does the editor seem to "get" you and your vision for the book? Do you understand each other well in writing and in conversation? Do the questions they ask about your work, either in conversation or in their sample edit, make it clear they're honoring your voice and your goals? Do you trust their ideas, and do you think they trust yours, too? Can you be straightforward and comfortable with this person?

I love what developmental editor Chantel Hamilton says about finding fit: "There's only so much we can guess about our own responses before we actually get into the work of editing, so be prepared to surprise yourself from time to time. Being edited is hard, and brave, and worth it…. The more honest you are with [your editor] about who you are and what you need, the better the process and the book will be."

# CHAPTER 3

# GETTING THE MOST OUT OF THE EDITORIAL EXPERIENCE

Once you've found an editor who's a great match and whom you trust to celebrate and elevate your work, I know you'll want to get the most out of the experience—for the sake of your current book and every future book you write. This chapter is full of tips and prompts to help you do just that.

On a practical level, you'll make the most of your editor's time and your money by cleaning up the manuscript as much as possible before handing it off, especially before language editing. This means attending to some of the low-level details yourself. Here's a quick checklist:

Read the manuscript out loud—or have software read it to you—to help catch the errors you're gliding right over when you're reading the text for the umpteenth time.

Put only one space between sentences.

Check online for lists of commonly mixed-up words and run your manuscript through the list.

Double-check your facts, names, and dates.

Look for incredibly long paragraphs and sentences. Break them into logical smaller ones so you don't exhaust your reader.

Make sure the manuscript is complete before a copyedit and proofread. This includes figures; image captions; quotes; and all the text that appears before and after the main body of the book, like the title page, dedication, notes, or glossary (known as *front* and *back matter*).

Put the manuscript in the format your editor requested. Thank you in advance!

I've been harping on it all book long, and I'm going to do it one more time: open communication is the key to getting what you need from this working relationship, at any and every point in your manuscript's life. That's why most of the conversation starters below are in the form of questions.

I invite you to use them as a checklist during your own revision process, too. They'll give you insight into your own writing and strengthen your manuscript before and after working with an editor.

## GETTING THE MOST OUT OF A DEVELOPMENTAL EDIT

The developmental editor holds your goals and intentions for the book in one hand, your manuscript in the other, and brings them up together in front of the light. Then they do the careful, clear-eyed work of showing you how to align the two. They are responding to your vision for what this book can be. But they're also on the hook for telling you whether or not you're achieving that vision, or if that vision sells your book short. They may even propose a different vision for the work—one they think will be more effective toward your goals, or a stronger offering in the market.

To do this work well, developmental editors first need to understand your vision. The conversation starters below will help you both come to that understanding together.

### Questions to Discuss with Your Developmental Editor

To help your editor understand your goals and intentions—and therefore let you get the most out of a developmental edit—I suggest you and your editor talk through questions like these.

> Do you plan to independently publish or traditionally publish? If the latter, do you already have an agent or a publisher? If not, are you aiming it toward a particular kind of publisher?

> Who is your intended audience, and how much do they know about your subject? What will they know or feel when they begin your book? Why might they be picking it up in the first place?

What do you want people to take away from your book? How do you want them to feel at the end? What do you want them to know and be able to do when they're done reading?

Why are you writing it? Why are you the right person to write it?

Are you writing to the conventions of a particular genre or field, or deliberately trying to stretch some boundaries or conventions?

What do you think are the current strengths and weaknesses of the manuscript?

The developmental editor is also a dynamic, empathetic bridge between you and your reader. In that role, they're considering the following as they work:

Is the book in the best order and arrangement to get your ideas across clearly?

Does the book say what you want it to say? Will the reader take away what you want them to?

What's special and working well about your book, and how can the editor help you bring more of that forward?

Do the structure and level of the writing match what your intended audience understands and is interested in?

Where are you giving the reader everything they need, and where are you assuming too much?

Are the sections of your manuscript weighted well in relation to each other? Or is one bloated with extra examples, say, or one lacking the argumentary heft of the others?

Are there holes in your argument or story? Sections of less energy where your reader could get confused or bored and put down the book?

Does the structure of your book support your credibility and trustworthiness as an author?

Does your book hang together as a whole?

Are you unintentionally trying to cram more than one book in here? If so, how can you pull them apart, which one will you choose to write first, and what's needed to fill it out?

I encourage you to go into this structural, developmental work as openly as possible. When you read the editorial memo and manuscript comments, let everything marinate for a few days before digging into revisions. Unless you're set aflame with insight and enthusiasm, in which case go go go!

If you feel defensive, give yourself a while to cool down and become less tender so you can consider the edits with a curious mind.

## GETTING THE MOST OUT
## OF A LANGUAGE EDIT

You cultivate a particular style as a writer-reviser. A language editor's job is to submerge ourselves halfway in that style so our edits sound and feel like you, not us. To do it well, it helps to know what's important to you about your own writing. You can help your editor—and get the most out of any language edit—by chatting in detail about style, voice, and goals before you begin. Here's one example of clear communication that sets a line edit up for success.

In 2022, I worked with a client on a manuscript she was about to send back to her publisher after a round of revisions. She asked me to line edit just the first chapter, which needed to be a strong opening for the book but hadn't yet been polished in the way she wanted. Her email was a dream to receive because of how clearly it laid out her preferences, goals, and needs. I used it as the rubric for each edit I considered proposing.

> I'm hoping that the highly detailed level of reporting will distinguish this book, so it's especially important to me to strip it of any cliché while making the characters and descriptions as vivid as possible. I'm also aware that the number of times I've reorganized this chapter...has probably led to some awkward transitions. So please keep an eye out for the movement between paragraphs to see whether I need to put [in some new transitions].
>
> I would also say regarding voice and style, I want the writing, especially in this chapter, to *move*. This is my moment to wrap the reader into the story and convince

> them to stick around.... I think the main character's story
> is compelling enough to do that...so if anything feels
> lacking I tend to think the solution is to look toward
> the reporting rather than trying to douse it in my own
> emotional commentary.

If you're not used to thinking about your own writing in this detail and depth, working with a line editor is the perfect chance to begin building that muscle. You'll become aware of your preferences as a writer. You'll also develop the attention and the skills you need to hone your craft and break yourself out of habits when necessary.

And sometimes breaking your habits is, in fact, necessary. Just because you love long sentences, for example, doesn't mean they're the right choice for the reader—or the right choice throughout a manuscript. If the reader can't follow you through those long sentences, the style choice is dragging down the book. If there's no variation in rhythm, your reader will get bored. A confused or bored reader puts down the book. So your editor should be able to work flexibly within your preferences as much as possible while pushing back against what isn't serving your writing, your ideas, or your reader.

Yes, you will see a lot of changes in the manuscript when you get a language edit back. Many marks from the digital red pen.

As hard as it may be not to prickle when someone exposes the innards of your work this way, try to remember that your editor is suggesting those changes in service of you, your reader, and your best possible book.

And at the end of the day, the final decision about whether or not to accept an editor's suggestion is always yours.

## Questions to Discuss with Your Language Editor

Here's a list of questions to guide your conversation with your language editor. Most are designed for line editing, but some of these questions are relevant to copyediting, too. (And you'll notice some partial overlap with developmental questions.) Having this conversation makes it more likely you'll get back a manuscript that sounds and feels true to you. It'll also minimize the number of times your editor has to pester you with questions in the middle of the process.

Do you have any strong habits or preferences on style, including tone, rhythm, word choice, and punctuation? Which of these do you think are useful, and which would you like your editor's help finding alternatives for?

What feelings or visceral responses are you trying to evoke, if any?

What are your desired rhythms for different sections of the book (as my client wanted the text to "move")?

Have you varied sentence length and word choice where appropriate to keep reader attention sharp?

Who is your intended audience? Are you speaking to them at a level they can understand, or are you overwhelming them with jargon or talking down to them?

Are you aiming to write within certain conventions of a genre or field, or do you want to purposefully break them? For example, you may want to write in a straightforward and approachable way even though most texts in your field are dense.

Does the language of your book support your credibility and trustworthiness as an author?

Think about whether you'd like your editor to suggest changes and leave every revision up to you to execute, or whether you'd prefer your editor to directly make many of the changes and explain their choices for you to review. Most editors default to somewhere in the middle, so talk with your editor to agree on an approach.

Remember when I said copyeditors make a style sheet, that list of style preferences, usage notes, and terms in your book? (See Dive 1 at the back of the book for an example.) If you have the bandwidth for it, you can save them time—and perhaps save yourself money if they charge by the hour—by compiling the beginnings of the sheet yourself. If there are special terms or lots of names in your book, give your editor a list with correct spellings. Triple-check those spellings. They'll check them, too. If you hate em dashes and don't want them in your book, write that down for your editor. If you hate em dashes and have persevered this far in my book anyway, thank you. Send me an email and I'm happy to talk about why I love them.

CHAPTER 4

# FEARS AND FAQs

## WHAT WILL ALL THIS COST ME?

I conducted many a poll while writing this book, and cost kept coming up as the number one fear for the majority of authors. Will getting my book edited cost an arm and a leg and a gold tooth? Worse, what if it costs that much *and* I hate what I get back?

We can take care of that last concern right now, because you've read this book.

Make use of the tips and conversation prompts within, and approach working with an editor as a booster rocket experience. If you do, you stand an excellent chance of being delighted by their edits, growing as a writer, and producing a book you truly love.

Now, onto the trickier bit.

The cost of editing depends on so many factors, and varies so much by editor and by level of editing, that a detailed discussion of cost is outside the purview of this book. But here are some ballpark basics. Independent editors set their own rates based on training and experience, your project timeline, the manuscript's genre, what the edit will entail, and their own business requirements. Some charge by the word, some by the hour, some by a flat project fee.

The Editorial Freelancers Association's rate chart (see Dive 4 at the back of this book) shares some average rates for all levels of editing. But you'll find plenty of variation outside the ranges they list, and being outside these ranges isn't necessarily a red flag. Coaches charge anything from $75/hour to $1,500/hour depending on their expertise, service, and market. For a full-length book manuscript, you can usually expect developmental editing on a finished draft to be somewhere around $3,000–$6,000. Language editing may be closer to $1,500–$4,000. The very lightest copyediting and proofreading may be $800–$1,500. But again, these are ballpark figures.

> An editor's cost is separate, too, from their worth. They bring years of experience and highly trained expertise to your work. They save you time, add inestimable value to the quality of your book, and help you produce a volume you can be personally and professionally proud of for years to come.

I recognize that paying to work with professionals is just not feasible for many writers. I'm not telling you that you must work with an editor at every stage of your manuscript's life or your work will inevitably flop. No editor has control over how your book does in the marketplace, and working with one or many doesn't guarantee success. But expectations in the commercial marketplace are high. Hiring at least one editor certainly increases the chances readers will keep reading after the first page, stay engaged to the end, and then recommend your book to others.

According to Corinne Jorgenson, the cognitive scientist, studies show texts that come across as "messy" are put down faster and are less persuasive (yes, there's systemic bias baked into this). Readers might not even get into the meat of your ideas if they're turned off by too many clunky sentences, grammatical mistakes, or typos. So if you only have room in your budget for one professional editor, make it a copyeditor. Some are willing to do a *proof-edit*, which combines elements of a light copyedit with a proofread.

If you can afford just a little more professional help, hire someone to assist you at the big-picture level with a developmental edit or even just a manuscript critique. If you can't hire help at this level, you must tend to the same concerns yourself. Everyone's disappointed if they open a beautiful package only to reveal a present that falls apart right away; don't let your arguments, ideas, or story be a shoddy present in a pretty package. Use the developmental editing considerations in Chapter 3 and patterns in your beta reader feedback to guide you as you revise carefully on your own.

## ARE YOU JUDGING ME?

Hillary Weiss Presswood is a powerhouse brand strategist who projects confidence like a disco ball. But in the middle of writing her first book she asked me an important, not-so-sparkly question: "Do you ever find yourself judging clients juuuust a teensy bit?"

I hear some version of this question often—most editors do— and I understand it completely. You've worked really hard. You generally like to be good at what you do. You certainly want to write a good book. And you've poured so much of yourself into your writing that sometimes your writing starts to feel like a part of you, so anyone criticizing your writing is criticizing *you*. That's painful. It's also not what's happening in the author-editor relationship.

> Here's the distinction I like to draw. I'm never judging, but I am using judgment all the time.

Passing judgment—as in to "criticize or condemn someone from a position of assumed moral superiority" (thanks, Merriam-Webster)—has absolutely no place in editing. It honestly doesn't occur to me. Not even a teensy bit.

But judgment *is* an essential part of an editor's job in the sense of informed discernment, "the ability to make considered decisions or come to sensible conclusions" (thanks again, Merriam-Webster). Editors make judgments on every page of your writing, about your writing, *so that we can draw out the best in it.* I want your book to be clearer and more persuasive after I edit it than it was when you passed it to me. Ideally, working with me will also help you level up your own writing and revision skills so you get better as a writer, project after project. My judgment works toward those ends.

But, as LeVar Burton used to say at the end of every *Reading Rainbow* episode, you don't have to take my word for it. So what do other editors have to say?

Kendra Olson emphasizes learnable skill instead of bad or good: "An author I worked with on a developmental edit expressed concern that her writing might not be any good. I told her that I tend to view writing as being more or less skillful; in other words, writing is a muscle that can be strengthened. The author-editor relationship plays an important role in this."

Editor and writing coach Sabrina Estudillo Butler puts it this way: "Writing is such an emotional process, even when you're not writing about something emotional. My job as your editor is not to judge you or make you feel bad about your mistakes—we all make those. I'm a teammate, here to assist you in making sure you're saying what you want to say in a way that the reader can understand and connect with. Your work deserves to be approached with curiosity and critiqued with compassionate candor, never judgment."

Language editor Claire Cronshaw says, "If it's the idea of accuracy that's scaring you, don't worry about it. Getting the accuracy right so the story can be enjoyed is where editors and proofreaders can help you. So bring your work to me without fear of embarrassment. I'm not judging you. An editor is not an examiner. An editor is not your teacher. Don't let school day hang-ups get in the way of your success."

## HOW DO I KNOW WHEN IT'S TIME TO LET GO?

Some writers can't wait to pass their work to an editor so they can stop looking at the damn thing. Others tinker and tinker and tinker, convinced it's never quite good enough; someone has to pry the manuscript out of their hands. Most folks are somewhere in the middle but wonder when it's the right time to pass the work off for a boost. So how do you know when it's time to stop working on your own—when it's "ready"?

Here's how you know it's *not* ready: if you haven't done at least one thorough, careful revision on your own, preferably more.

But it is ready if you think it's as good as you can get it without help, and you want it to be better. It's ready if you aren't sure what to do next or even whether the darn thing is making sense to other people. It's ready if you think the next step is one in which you don't have as much skill—like if you're a big-picture thinker but you need help lining up all the little details to support that big picture. It's ready if you feel you just can't "see" it anymore. It's definitely ready if you've started to worry that your revisions are actually making things worse or sucking the life out of your writing.

There's a sneaky second question here: When are *you* ready to hand the manuscript off to an editor? If you're having trouble separating yourself from the manuscript—you can see the document is ready to go but you're not emotionally ready to let it go—take a deep breath. Why aren't you ready? Would it help to reread the section on judgment above? Consider talking through the why of this with a friend or colleague whom you trust not to tease or shame you, but to listen, help you explore, and invite you to let go.

If you've read this book and put in the effort to find an editor you click with, I hope you will let yourself take the leap, trusting your editor to handle your work with respect and care. A good editor is rooting for your work and for you, doing their best to enliven your book and make you look great in the process. And, yet again, I encourage you to communicate with your editor. Feeling nervous? Tell them. They may suggest a tweak to their working process, like a midway check-in, that will help set you at ease.

## HOW DO I KNOW WHAT YOU'VE CHANGED IN MY MANUSCRIPT?

Most editors prefer to receive files in Microsoft Word, and will use its Track Changes feature to show you their changes. This tool lets you, the author, control how much of the editorial work you see by hiding and revealing different types of edits without deleting them. Editors also leave you comments in the margin, called *queries*. These queries may pose questions, discuss revision options, or explain their edits. Some editors are also comfortable working in Google Docs, using its Suggest and Comment features, but it's uncommon for books because editors use many software tools that don't run on Google Docs. Proofreaders may work with final layouts formatted as Adobe PDFs; they'll usually leave comment bubbles and markup in the document to record their work.

No matter the format, you get to accept or reject each edit and revise as desired. At the end of the day, this is your manuscript and we want you to be happy with it. The final decision is always yours.

If you're unfamiliar with or overwhelmed by Track Changes, search primers online, ask your own editor for help, or access my quick how-to guide via Dive 4 at the back of this book.

## WILL YOU RIP THE HEART OUT OF MY BOOK AND MAKE IT SOUND LIKE SOMEONE ELSE?

I'll tell it to you straight: there are some editors out there who are more concerned with their vision and voice than with yours. They might very well smother your book or tear its heart out. But the editor who will do that is, frankly, not good at their job. A good editor will speak up thoughtfully and straightforwardly when they think your preferences are holding your manuscript back, while honoring your style and making the best of your voice shine.

This is one reason why the initial emails and conversations with a potential editor, their testimonials, and the sample edit are so important. Do you like how the editor treats you? Treats your manuscript? How they ask questions and phrase their suggestions? If not, it's OK to move on and find someone else who will take better care of your work. With the questions and recommendations laid out in this book, you now have the power to find the right editor for you—one who will strengthen your book's heart, rather than rip it out.

# YOU CAN DO THIS

Working with an editor takes vulnerability—both in handing it off and in getting it back. Processing your editor's feedback can feel emotionally and intellectually overwhelming. Take breaks when you need to. Remember the editor is on your side, even if it doesn't always feel that way in a moment of self-protection.

I hope that by sticking with it you'll come to enjoy the editorial process as mighty nourishment—an opportunity for fresh curiosity, energy, and insight that will make your book better than you ever imagined it could be.

# Resources for a
# Deeper Dive

# SEE FOR YOURSELF: EDITING EXAMPLES

## EXAMPLE DEVELOPMENTAL EDIT

Susan Cain is a bestselling author. Her first book, *Quiet: The Power of Introverts in a World That Can't Stop Talking*, was named one of the best books of the year by institutions from *Library Journal* to *O, The Oprah Magazine*.

But before the book became a smash hit, it was a "terrible" draft. And she was lucky enough to have an editor at Crown Publishing Group, Peter Guzzardi, who saw the potential in the draft and in Susan's ideas and helped her turn the manuscript into a stellar book. (She also had the gift of a publisher giving her the time to get it right.)

What follows is an excerpt of one of Peter's developmental revision letters (aka editorial memos) to Susan. A good developmental editor balances honest enthusiasm and encouragement with straightforward clarity about how the book can change for the better—and can respectfully communicate how to take it there. This letter is a masterful example of that balance.

Susan offers this contextualizing note:

> About two years after I signed a contract to write *Quiet*, I turned in a draft of the book, more or less on deadline— yay for me! Except that the draft was terrible. I knew this—and as soon as my editors read it, they knew it too. If you have a creative work you're trying to perfect, you're probably going to mess up along the way, too. AND THIS IS PART OF THE PROCESS—REALLY.
>
> *Quiet* spent seven years on the *New York Times* bestseller list. It has sold over four million copies and was translated into over forty languages. But this is what it looked like along the way.

### Editorial Memo

> Dear Susan,
>
> As we discussed, you've come up with a really exciting, ambitious book idea, which has the potential to be one of those books that everyone's talking about, that truly has an impact on the way we see ourselves, each other, and the world....
>
> The bad news is that there's no easy way to write a book with such expansive aspirations. It's going to take more work than a book that follows the beaten path. Lots more.

Specifically, this means completely rewriting this first draft. But, as we've discussed, I know you have the talent to do it, Crown is giving you time to do what needs to be done, and the topic you've chosen is so interesting that it inspires us all. The rest is a matter of structure and execution—no small challenge, but certainly one that's within reach.

When I was reading this first draft, I lit up with excitement in places that may give us insight into areas of emphasis for the second draft.... The notion that we've created a dichotomy out of introversion/extroversion, where we're probably all a little of both, was intriguing to me. I wanted to know much more about that. The Person/Situation Debate seems like an interesting way in to the subject, although we're really looking at a spectrum of personality within the "Person" half of that split, as opposed to exploring whether or not people have fixed aspects of their personalities. I was also thoroughly intrigued by your comment on page 51 that "introversion/extroversion is today the most studied personality variable after IQ, with hundreds of researchers devoting their entire careers to it." Why? What are they hoping to find? The answers to those questions might lie at the heart of this book.

As you know, Rachel and I both found ourselves hoping for more science in this book. I felt the absence of the two science chapters listed in the Table of Contents of the original proposal, particularly with regard to serotonin, and its inherent promise that we'd be exploring neurotransmitters and the mysteries of the brain. You won't be surprised to hear that my favorite chapter in the first draft is "This Is Your Brain on Small Talk." It supported my notion that there needed to be much more scientific research in this book, and also underscored one of the limitations of the tone of this book, which I think of as its "softness."

I'd like the prose to be tighter, crisper, more energetic, and more filled with information and excitement. After talking to you I think all those qualities are present in your ideas, it's just a matter of making sure that translates onto the page. Having lots of interesting research tidbits studded throughout the book to support and illustrate the various points you're making will certainly move us toward that end. As part of our shift toward putting a greater emphasis on research, we can include more stories about the psychological and sociological work being done on introversion and extroversion, and about the people who undertake that work—and perhaps are even its research subjects. (Currently most stories are about notable introverts.) We can also make the stories shorter and sharper.

I thought one of the most important aspects of our conversation was the part when I told you I was hoping for more science, and you said that your first instinct was to include a lot more, but you were concerned that research might make this book too demanding for the audience that turns out for hardcover bestsellers. As I told you last week, I really don't think that's a problem. Readers who made Gladwell and Gilbert's books big bestsellers are comfortable dealing with lots of complex information. They will be able to follow us wherever we can take them, in my opinion.

Reading this first draft I was struck by the notion that you're underselling what this book offers the reader. On manuscript pages 19 and 41, where you're summarizing the preface and the first chapter, you talk about this book being a call to arms, and an antidote to the Extrovert Ethic. By contrast to the ambitious promise of the book's subtitle those seem like modest aspirations. For one thing, they're pretty abstract, and even though this is not a self-help book I think readers want some take-away value that directly applies to their own lives. After reading these pages and talking to you I'm imagining a book with far more immediate impact than you've indicated on the page....

To my way of thinking, this book is not so much a call to arms as it is a whack on the side of the head.... So I think you need to raise the stakes here, first in your own mind, perhaps, and then on the page....

I do think that one of the challenges here is that once we accept the premise of the book (which is clearly expressed in the subtitle) the material runs the danger of being so patently obvious that it doesn't sustain the reader's interest. So when you're researching this topic I think you'll want to put a premium on examples and bits of information that are cool, or funny, or surprising. We're going to need to keep this lively. Surprise us.

By and large I think that in this first draft you, the author, are a bit too much with your readers. It's not that I don't want to know about you. I do. I want to know how you came to write this book, and why, and what qualifies you to do so. I want to know if you have sufficient expertise on the topic, or skill in describing it, to earn my trust. But I may want to get most of this information in the preface to the book. If I find myself reading too many stories about you, I begin to wonder if this is just stuff you've made up as you went along....

This means that I'm going to be leery about hearing too much about how you did your research. I don't want to hear too much about how you created the flying idea machine. I think this also means being careful about using terms of your own devising. Is Extrovert Ethic yours, for example...?

I hope that in my fervor to provide you with helpful suggestions I haven't drowned out my enthusiasm for the wonderful topic you've chosen, Susan, and your obvious skills as a wordsmith. I'm a fan, and I see the potential for a fascinating and very successful book here.

I'm in Chapel Hill until Sunday if you have any questions. My office phone is X, and my cell is Y.

And I'm generally responsive to email.

With warm regards,

Peter Guzzardi

# EXAMPLE LINE EDIT

Dr. Olson Pook specializes in editing complex ideas and turning them into comprehensible and engaging writing. He usually works iteratively and collaboratively, asking many rounds of questions of the writer as he helps clarify their ideas and uncover layer after layer of depth in the text.

This is a snapshot of one line edit. It shows Olson's first pass through the manuscript, where he was beginning to draw out the narrative thread of the work. After what you see here, he went through the manuscript several more times, pulling out other details and information to make the story behind the research shine.

## Original Version

Ramazan complained that during the Soviet period, there had been fire crews and trucks the likes of which could have helped.

In this arid steppe, fires are common events that threaten the income and livelihood of the residents. The seemingly random placement of haystacks that dot landscape and fueled the blaze, aren't at all. Koyaners selectively harvest from the once Soviet agricultural fields of wheat and other grasses—thousands of acres plots that some of the older residents had worked while nuclear testing was occurring simultaneously.

Earlier that day, on an otherwise clear morning—save for the rising columns of smoke—and at Ramazan's insistence, we drove across the fields toward the fire line to assess the damage in my old Mitsubishi Delica van, which happened to be the only functioning car the village had. Luckily, one of the villagers had bartered for diesel, either from a mine where they pick shifts or from a neighboring village. As we reached a small hill, we could see the grass steadily burning in all directions. High winds lifted embers, carrying them everywhere. Others were scanning the damage and preparing to act. Preventing a repeat of the previous year, in which some one hundred cows, an entire herd belonging to two families, starved to death, was the only priority. With sheepskins attached to long poles, in a region where water is scarce and there is no fire department, we began to fight the blazes in the only way possible—by snuffing them out. "The Delica" became a fire truck. We packed ourselves in with the steel milk drums sloshing water all over the inside of the car and drove from one fire line to the next, late into the night.

Although our fire brigade seemed effective—given that we were left to deal with the problem on our own—I was scared. This blaze, only the first one of 2010, would pass right through the nuclear test site. This is when

I realized that the boundaries, represented clearly on a map hanging in my one-room house in Koyan, meant absolutely nothing. Neither fire nor radioactive particles obey borders. Every time we hit the flame with our sheepskins or ran through the charred earth toward the next fire line, we crossed in and out the old atomic site. But no one really knew when because there were no signs or fences to warn us. I imagined radioactive particles—buried somewhere in layers of ash—re-suspended in the air once again, covering our clothes and drawing into our lungs.

## Edited Version

In this arid steppe, fires are common events that threaten the income and livelihood of the residents. The seemingly random placement of haystacks that dot the landscape and fuel the blaze isn't random at all. Koyaners selectively harvest wheat and other grasses from the former Soviet agricultural fields—thousands of acres that some of the older residents had worked while nearby nuclear tests were simultaneously occurring.

On an otherwise clear morning save for the rising columns of smoke, we drove across the fields toward the fire line to assess the damage in the only functioning car the village had: my old Mitsubishi Delica van. As we picked our way toward the burning horizon, Ramazan complained that during the Soviet era there had been fire crews and trucks. As it was, we were lucky that one of the villagers had bartered for diesel so that we had fuel.

Reaching a small hill, we could see the grass steadily burning in all directions, the high winds lifting embers and carrying them everywhere. Others had already arrived and were preparing to act. The only priority was preventing a repeat of the previous year's losses in which a herd of over one hundred cows died, having starved to death as a result of a food shortage caused by a similar conflagration. Without a fire department, we began to fight the blazes in the only way possible—by snuffing them out with sheepskins attached to long poles. We had packed the van with steel milk drums filled with water and drove the sloshing containers from one fire line to the next late into the night. The Delica became a makeshift fire truck.

Although our fire brigade seemed effective, I was scared about something else. This blaze—the first of many that summer—would pass right through the nuclear test site. Its boundaries, so clearly represented on the map hanging in my one-room apartment in Koyan, were meaningless out here. Neither fire nor radioactive particles obey borders. Every time we hit the flame with our sheepskins or ran through the charred earth toward the next fire line, we crossed in and out of the old atomic site. There were no signs or fences to warn us, and I imagined radioactive particles, buried long ago in layers of ash, reemerging once again to cover our clothes and enter our lungs.

# EXAMPLE COPYEDIT

Below is an excerpt from *Embers of Hope: Embracing Life in an Age of Ecological Destruction and Climate Chaos* by Bonita Eloise Ford. It was copyedited by Chelle Parker, who edits both fiction and nonfiction with a particular focus on supporting writers from demographics that are typically underrepresented in the publishing industry.

Here you'll see what a manuscript looks like when peppered with queries (those marginal notes) and changes via Microsoft Word's Track Changes. In this example, all Chelle's edits are visible. But if it looks overwhelming, don't worry—you don't *have* to look at this much information when you first get your manuscript back. You can choose to see everything, just the queries, or a totally clean version with no marks at all. (See Dive 4 for more on navigating Track Changes.)

**Acceptance and Change**

We cannot control what life brings. The Buddha taught that sickness, aging, and death are inevitable. Nonetheless, we can make the most of what we have.

> M Parker
> Serial comma, per style sheet.

When I asked Frank, my friend Katherine's husband, about how they coped with her illness, he explained a concept that comes from Buddhist teachings. He raised one hand in front of him: "This is how things are." He raised his second hand and held it a few inches from the first: "This is how you want things to be. The distance between the hands is your suffering." The more we resist the way things are, the more we fuel our discontent.

As a gardener, although I can nurture the seeds I've sown, I know there are many factors that I do not control. In permaculture design, we learn to work *with* nature rather than *against* it. We start with what exists and use it to create something that enhances life.

> M Parker
> Deleted: ,

A low-lying wet area may be the ideal spot for a pond. We might amplify existing conditions to provide something useful to us, like creating windbreaks to channel the wind towards a turbine.

> M Parker
> Since attribution is possible for this, we should include it.

What are the current conditions? Can we change them? What are the benefits of changing things compared to keeping things as they are? How much energy would it take to affect change and is it worth it?

> M Parker                                    Febr
> Did a quick fact-check on the phrasing here and adjusted accordingly.

> M Parker
> Deleted: think

I am reminded of American theologian Reinhold Niebuhr's Serenity Prayer: "God grant me the peace to accept the things I cannot change, the courage to change the things I can, and the wisdom to know the difference." We can think of a continuum: on one end, we accept life just as it is, and on the other end, we have agency to change things. Depending on the situation, some combination may serve us well.

> M Parker
> Deleted: the

> M Parker
> Deleted: p

> M Parker
> Deleted: ,

> M Parker
> Deleted: Please

Despite our concerns about life on Earth, it can still be helpful to start with acceptance—however, this does not mean being passive or giving up. To fight against something uses precious energy, whereas starting from and working with what already exists allows us to be more efficient. If we find ourselves in a strong current in the middle of a river, rather than resisting it, it is easier to move to the edge where the water is less turbulent, and then redirect our course towards where we want to go.

As we explore opportunities in the present moment and aim towards a greater vision, we foster new possibilities for the future….

## Self-Defeating Thoughts

Almost all of us make life harder for ourselves in some way. When we don't like past or present circumstances, we complain. We also ruminate over how things could go wrong in the future.

In *Living in the Light of Death: On the Art of Being Truly Alive*, Buddhist teacher Larry Rosenberg describes the Buddha's teaching about the two arrows: we all get hit by the "first arrow," which could be pain, sickness, aging, or death; there is no preventing this. The "second arrow," however, is the additional suffering that is created by the stories we tell ourselves and the emotional roller coasters we set in motion. The first arrow is not within our control, but the second arrow is. Although it may take a lot of practice, by becoming aware of these second arrows, we can learn to put them down.

Sometimes there is nothing inherently harmful or unpleasant about an external situation. When we let go of our inner dramas, we may find that the unpleasantness was created by our minds.

\*\*\*

I had been wanting to visit Thailand for as long as I've known Bastou. Finally, in [year], we were going to go. While there, we planned to attend a 10-day silent meditation retreat. I was very nervous about attending even though I thought it would be good for me.

Once we arrived in Thailand, I tried to meditate regularly to practice. One day at dusk, while meditating on the balcony of our hotel room, the mosquitoes started swarming around me. I flailed my arms to fend them off, then lost patience and went inside under the mosquito net to finish my meditation. I realised immediately that I wouldn't be able to do that during the retreat.

As we visited the monastery the day before the retreat began, I sat on a rock, admiring the well-kept grounds. Several mosquitoes found me. Bastou and I walked beyond the monastery gates, where there were fewer trees and mosquitoes, but still they found me. I cried. I didn't think I could tolerate 10 days of being bitten.

That night in the dorm, I had my first experience sleeping on a concrete bed. It offered only a very thin bamboo mat and a wooden pillow for comfort. Lying on my back, my tailbone hurt; lying on my side, my hip bones and neck ached. I barely slept.

I really wondered if I should leave. I thought, "Some people can do this. Some people can go with the flow, but I can't. I'm gonna freak out. The mosquitoes are crazy, the concrete bed hurts, and I can't meditate for the whole day. I'm gonna lose it. And then they'll tell me, 'Sorry, it would be best for everyone if you left.' I'll be stuck in the countryside with nowhere to go and I don't speak the language. I should just leave now before things get worse." My thoughts and feelings spun. Second arrows flew in every direction.

# EXAMPLE STYLE SHEET

Whether they work independently or for a publisher, your copyeditor will make a style sheet for your book. It collects in one place the author's and publisher's style preferences, the copyeditor's decisions, and a list of the book's specific terms. The style sheet then becomes a reference document that travels with your manuscript through the rest of the publication process, keeping everyone consistent and correct. It's used by the publisher in creating the final product and by the proofreader as they do that final check before the book goes to print.

This style sheet was created by bilingual editor Sofía Jarrín of Bilingual Libélula Editorial and Translation Services, who works with international journals and academic publishers in the United States and Latin America.

## Style Sheet

**Manuscript:** XXX
**Author:** XXX
**Publisher:** XXX

**Service:** Copyediting
Editing of writing for grammar, punctuation, sentence structure, consistency, typos, and citation formatting

**Citation Style:**
- Chicago Manual of Style (CMS), 17th edition
- Merriam-Webster's Dictionary, free version found at https://www.merriam-webster.com

**Publisher Style Guide:**

- None provided

**General Style:**

- Oxford serial comma: Y
- CMS 7.89 for hyphenation of compounds.
- CMS 7.16 for possessives: The possessive of most singular nouns is formed by adding an apostrophe and an s. The possessive of plural nouns is formed by adding an apostrophe only.

**Spanish Words and Translations:**

- Keep accents for all names and words in Spanish.
- Exceptions: Peru
- CMS 11.3 for italics of foreign words. Italicized only on its first occurrence.
- Diccionario de la lengua española: https://dle.rae.es/

**Numbers:**

- Centuries: nineteenth century (n.), nineteenth-century (adj.), mid twenty-first century
- Chapters: chapter 4
- Dates: date-month-year format (e.g., 6 May 2021)
- Decades: 1960s, 2010s
- Numbers 1–9: spelled out, except when referring to data or measurements (e.g., she was three years old; it measured 3 pixels by 4 pixels)
- Numbers 10+: numerals
- Numbers, ordinals: spelled out (e.g., twentieth)
- Percentages: 10 percent

**Punctuation:**

- Oxford comma: Y
- Periods for common abbreviations?: N (US, UN)

**Table of Abbreviations:**

ALAS — Asociación LatinoAmérica-Suiza

APCOB — Apoyo para el Campesino-Indígena del Oriente Boliviano (Aid to the Indigenous Peasantry of Eastern Bolivia)

CEJIS — Centro de Estudios Jurídicos e Investigación Social (Center for Legal Studies and Social Research)

TIPNIS — Isiboro Sécure National Park and Indigenous Territory

**Spelling of Names, Places, and Terminology:**

A
Agrarian Reform Decree of 1953
*agregados* (foreigners)
Almaraz, Alejandro
Áñez, Jeanine
Arce, Luis
*arrimantes*
Atahualpa
Ayaviri, Alonso

B
Balcazar, Gregorio
Ballivián, General Hugo
Banco Agrícola de Bolivia
Bánzer Suárez, General Hugo

C
*cacique* (indigenous leader)
*caciques apoderados* (communal leaders)
Cajamarca
Calla, Ricardo
Chaco War
*cocaleros* (coca growers)
*colonato*
*colonizadores* (peasant migrants of the lowlands)
*colonos* (indentured servants)
Colque, Gonzalo
*composiciones de tierras* ("unoccupied" lands)
*comunarios* (former members of indigenous communities)

D
Díaz, Porfirio

E
*encomendero(s)* (Spanish in
    charge of encomiendas)
*encomienda(s)* (Spanish in
    charge of encomiendas)

F
First National Indigenous
    Congress
*forasteros*
Frías, Tomás

G
García Meza, Luis
Gotkowitz, Laura
Grajeda, Hilario
Grey Postero, Nancy
Grisaffi, Thomas
*guayras* (melting furnace)
Guevara Arce, Walter
Gutiérrez, Tomás Monje

H
*hacienda* (large estate)
Hearst, William Randolph
Hertzog, José Enrique

I
ILO Convention Concerning
    Indigenous and Tribal
    Peoples, 1989, No. 169

"Indian" (uppercase, for use
    by Spanish colonists)
Indigenista Interamerican
    Institute (Instituto
    Indigenista Interamericano)
indigenous (lowercase for
    use any other time)
Interamerican Indigenista
    Congress

K
Klein, Herbert S.

L
*latifundio/latifundios*
Lavaud, Jean Pierre
Ley del Instituto Nacional de
    Reforma Agraria
Ley de Reconducción
    Comunitaria
Loayza, Román

M
Machaca, Jesús de
*mallku* (indigenous authority)
Mariátegui, José Carlos
Marinković, Branko
*mita* (forced labor)
*mitayo* (indigenous workers)
Mohoza
Molina, Ramiro
Montes, Ismael

O
Omasuyos

P
Pando, José Manuel
Pizarro, Francisco
Platt, Tristan
*pongueaje*
Potosí

Q
*queñua* (native tree)
Quevedo, Luis Ramos
Quintanilla, Carlos

R
Real Audiencia of Charcas
*reducciones* (towns
    established around a
    square, a church, and a
    town hall)
*repartimiento* (forced
    distribution/sale of goods)
republican (lowercase,
    favoring, supporting, or
    advocating a republic)
Richardson Construction
    Company
Robins, Nicholas

S
Saignes, Thierry
Sánchez de Lozada, Gonzalo
Semo, Enrique
Siles Zuazo, Hernán
*Sitiajeros*
Soruco, Ximena
Sucre, Antonio José de

T
Taraco
Tarija
Terrazas, Luis
Thiesenhusen, William C.
Tierra Comunitaria de Origen

U
Ucureña
Upper Peru
Urriolagoitía, Mamerto

V
Viceroyalty of Peru
Villarroel, Gualberto

W
Wesz, Valdemar João

Y
*yanaperos*

Z
Zaballa, Eguino
Zárate Willka, Pablo

# SIX EASY PATHS TO CONNECTION AND SUPPORT

Way back in the introduction, I shared a story about open-door coworking evenings with my husband and our friends. A similar feeling of community and connection is possible for you as you work on your book. Partnering with a writing or book coach will certainly help you feel less alone. Working with an editor you enjoy will bring some of this energy, too.

> But you deserve this kind of support throughout the entire writing process; you don't have to wait for a professional to get it.

Take a moment to think through your own community and support systems. Who holds you up while you're writing? Who is your accountability buddy? Who can help you generate momentum or energy when you feel fresh out and have for days, weeks, months? Who cheers you on and reassures you that you can, in fact, write? Who helps you see the way through when you're stuck?

If you don't have ready answers or are looking for fresh ideas, here are six simple ways you can connect with others. Inspiration, not prescription. Let them nourish you and your writing, for this book and for the long haul of your creative life.

- Host a writing or coworking event for a group of friends or colleagues, like our grading nights. It doesn't have to be all writers, and it doesn't have to be in person.

- Join a community of fellow writers online, like the Nonfiction Authors Association (paid), Women in Publishing School (paid), or a local writers Discord or Facebook group (free). If you're in the Philadelphia, PA, area, contact me for an invite to a fantastically active and supportive Discord.

- Join a regularly scheduled online writing session, like Team Moxie Power Hour (paid) or A Very Important Meeting (free), so writing time is booked into your calendar. Take this time seriously.

- Ask a buddy if you can text them at the end of every day or every week with your word count or a note about a writing-related task you've accomplished. They respond with a celebratory emoji. Done.

- Exchange draft readings with a peer.

Schedule regular time in your calendar to feed your writing craft. Poke around websites like LitHub or read newsletters on craft and process, like Nicole Chung's "I Have Notes" at *The Atlantic*. Reading across genres, thinking deeply about reading and writing, and engaging with critical essays can build skill, generate sparks, and help us feel a part of a network of thinkers rather than a solitary laborer in the void.

# FOUR REVISION TIPS TO KEEP YOUR READERS ENTHRALLED— RIGHT TO THE LAST PAGE

Effective nonfiction writing rolls out the welcome mat for your reader and keeps them comfortable the whole way through. If you're writing informational or narrative nonfiction, you want your reader to trust you enough to engage with your ideas, understand those ideas, and find your work enjoyable from beginning to end. Trust comes partly from your credentials and those of your sources. But in an immediate, felt sense, it also comes from the clarity and coherence of your writing.

When you give readers all the information needed to enter into your world, in the order it's most easily assimilated, they can relax, absorb, and engage responsively with your ideas. You're welcoming them. Taking care of them. Giving them everything they need to get up close with your work and be fascinated.

But when you make readers backtrack to the previous page to remember what you're talking about, stop to puzzle out tricky sentence constructions, or spend a while wondering why you're bringing something up, you're making them work too hard. You're yanking them out of your spell, breaking that sense of care and trust—and giving them an opportunity to shift their attention elsewhere.

Many drafts that come to me for developmental or line editing accidentally push readers away. So let's talk about four strategies you can use while revising to roll out the welcome mat, pull people in, and keep them engaged all the way through your book. (They apply to shorter pieces of writing, too.)

## 1. CHOOSE WORDS THAT INVITE YOUR READER IN

Obfuscation—excessively fancy words, purposefully complex sentences, unnecessary technical jargon—keeps your readers away from your ideas. Many academic disciplines seem to live and die by obscurantist prose, and you might feel a professional need to fit in. (I'm not on board, but I'm an editor, not an academic—though you now know I'm married to one.) Keeping the reader out, or keeping the reader in suspense, may be appropriate techniques for some forms of creative nonfiction. But the purpose of much nonfiction is to inform, so choose words and sentence structures that help your reader get informed. Welcoming your reader into your prose also welcomes them to your ideas, helping them "get it" faster and more deeply.

This is definitely not a call to oversimplify or deaden your writing, or to make it patronizing or hand-holdy! Welcoming writing is often the most beautiful. The straightforward is not always simple. Surprises, silliness, playing with the timeline, layering mini essays, or interweaving ideas can be welcoming when carefully crafted with the reader in mind. As you revise, aim for word choice and sentence structure that are approachable and straightforward without sacrificing interest and intent.

Bonus: a reader who understands and is interested in your work is more likely to share it with other readers.

## 2. SUPPORT THE REAL POINT

Most writers I know are overwriters. You just keep writing, writing, writing—many more words than you need—until all your ideas are on the page. Then you edit it down later. It's a great technique. I'm an overwriter and a firm believer in the power and importance of terrible drafts. What a relief not to have to get it exactly right the first time!

Being an overwriter means you often don't discover the magical thing you're really trying to say until you've finished writing your first—or fourth—draft.

Here's the trick: once you discover what you're really trying to say, you have to go back through your manuscript and revise so that the text prepares for, supports, and follows from that point. Not from what you thought your point was when you started the draft.

I know, I know, you're sick of your manuscript already. But don't skip this step! Your reader needs it if they're going to understand your insights. A developmental or line editor can help you with this if you're having trouble on your own.

## 3. GIVE YOUR READERS A GROCERY CART

People assimilate information better when it connects to something they already know and when they understand *why* you're telling them something. For informational writing, make sure that you've shared both your topic (what you're talking about) and your point (what you want to say about it) close to the beginning of each relevant section.

Sometimes you go to the grocery store to pick up just one or two things and decide you don't need a cart. But as you go through the aisles you end up getting more and more and suddenly your arms are full, a box of cereal just thwapped on the floor, and you realize you really should have gotten a cart after all. Don't let your readers feel this way about the pieces of information you're giving them. Instead, give them a conceptual cart as soon as they enter the store, so they have a way to hold and understand all the details.

Two of the easiest ways to tell readers what to expect are *metadiscourse* (a fancy word for signals like: "In this chapter I'll show that...") and its subset, *signposting* ("I have three arguments about this"), which help articulate the structure of a piece of writing and ease the reader's way through. But I generally encourage a very light and careful hand with these kinds of obvious markers in non-academic prose because they can break the flow and spell of your writing. Sometimes they themselves even push readers out.

So instead of "This chapter covers the factors that cause brands to rise and fall in popularity," consider: "What makes a brand's popularity rise and fall?" Instead of "The first topic to be discussed is the motivation for Smith's actions," try diving right into it with something like: "Smith never shied away from discussing his motivations in public."

As Steven Pinker writes in *The Sense of Style*, "The problem with thoughtless signposting is that the reader has to put more work into understanding the signposts than she saves in seeing what they point to, like complicated directions for a shortcut which take longer to figure out than the time the shortcut would save. It's better if the route is clearly enough laid out that every turn is obvious when you get to it."

## 4. CHECK WITH YOUR AUDIENCE

Try to imagine yourself as one of your ideal readers. How explicitly you have to describe the connections between ideas depends in part on your intended audience and how much they know. Keep in mind that they probably know less than you think. You understand your material inside out and backward, but even expert readers haven't been living inside your brain. They won't know everything you do about your unique take on the topic. Chances are good that you need more explicit explanations and transitions than you think you do.

Once you've imagined and revised for that intended reader, find at least one real human in your audience and ask them to read the manuscript. Have them flag where they stumble, get confused, or tune out. Better yet, ask for feedback from at least six beta readers—people in your ideal audience who are not your family or close friends. Try not to be derailed by just one person's pointed opinion. Rather, revise in response to comments that truly resonate with you or to the patterns you see within all the feedback.

If you're not able to get the text in front of someone else, read it aloud to yourself or have software read it to you. Note every place you trip over your words or something doesn't make sense, then go back in and see if you can figure out why. How can you rearrange information, provide something new, delete something irrelevant, or tinker with the transitions to smooth out the flow and help your reader understand absolutely everything? Hearing the text aloud is the best way to catch typos and missing words, too—so you can return to this technique again and again as you refine your manuscript.

# MORE RESOURCES TO SUPPORT YOUR BOOK JOURNEY

ast dive of the book! Visit https://www.hannahdk.com/how-to-enjoy-being-edited/resources to find a treasure chest of resources that will deepen your knowledge, expand your tool kit, and ease your work with publishing professionals. You'll find gems like:

- Links to the searchable membership databases of professional editorial associations

- Recommendations for books that will help you strengthen your writing and revision craft

- The Editorial Freelancers Association rate chart

- Guides to different publishing paths and to working with other book professionals

- And much more

Happy reading, and happy writing.

# ACKNOWLEDGMENTS

A trapeze twirl of gratitude to fellow book coach Vicky Quinn Fraser, whose public championing of microbooks gave me the confidence to call my writing a book in the first place.

My beta readers' thoughtful engagement with the manuscript blew me away. Thank you so much, J.V. Fahl, Leonid Korogodski, Johanna McWeeney, Jackie Raymond, Kathy Soulsby, and Casey von Neumann.

Thanks to copyeditor Lauren Alexander of Scribe & Sunshine, whose vibe I respected immediately (and yes, I still asked for a sample edit). I'm so glad I could rely on your perceptive edits to tease out my snarly sentences and make this sucker shine.

Many thanks to the authors and editors who shared their work and words to make this book as useful as possible.

And thanks to my family, for your unquestioning confidence I could do this. What a gift.

# ABOUT THE AUTHOR

Hannah de Keijzer (deh-KAI-zer...it's easier than it looks) was that nerdy high school student who owned and regularly referenced an etymological dictionary. Now she channels that nerdom as an editor and proofreader who helps authors craft standout writing that's clear and compelling to their ideal audience.

Her clients publish independently or traditionally at places like Cornell University Press, Cambridge University Press, and W. W. Norton. She's an active member of the Editorial Freelancers Association and ACES: The Society for Editing. And yes, that dictionary still lives right next to her desk.

As a writing coach, Hannah helps clients get words on the page when they're stuck or overwhelmed, design and stay on track with realistic ways of reaching their goals, and build a sustainable writing practice that fits their particular brain and busy life—so their books and other projects get *done*. With ease, momentum, and fun, no less!

Hannah built her chops in creative collaboration over a decade as a professional performing artist and co-artistic director of a dance company. When not working with words, you'll find her dancing, creating wild and asymmetrical flower bouquets, basking in patches of sunshine like a sleepy dog, and hiking with her family.

Get in touch via her website, www.hannahdk.com, or email her at hannah@hannahdk.com to ask follow-up questions about anything in this guide or to start a conversation about how editing or coaching can galvanize your own book process.

# THANK YOU!

THANK YOU FOR READING MY BOOK.

I APPRECIATE IT, AND YOU.

I f you'd like to hear more from me, sign up for my newsletter (occasional typos and all) at www.hannahdk.com. I send missives twice a month about writing, revision, editing, how to help your body and workspace serve as fuel for creative work, and building a sustainable writing practice. I also post regularly on LinkedIn.

If you have questions about what's in this book or would like to work with me to bring yours into being, I would love to get to know you and your writing. Just send me an email at hannah@hannahdk .com to say hello.

If you'd like to share your thoughts about this book with other writers, please consider leaving a review. Reviews and personal recommendations are essential information for potential new readers and essential currency for authors.

And if this guide was a useful helping hand to you along the journey to publication, email me when your book is available for purchase so I can help you spread the word. I can't wait to see your book in the world!

www.ingramcontent.com/pod-product-compliance
Lightning Source LLC
Chambersburg PA
CBHW022103020426
42335CB00012B/812